THE USBORNE
ASTRONAUT'S
HANDBOOK

Written by Louie Stowell

Illustrated by Roger Simo

With additional illustrations by
Adam Larkum & Jamie Ball

Foreword by European Space Agency
astronaut Tim Peake

CONTENTS

Foreword

SO YOU WANT TO BECOME AN ASTRONAUT?

Well then, this guide is a really great place to start – but there are many different paths you could take to get to space.

I was a test pilot before being selected by the European Space Agency for astronaut training. My fellow astronauts all come from different countries and had jobs such as scientists, engineers, doctors and pilots.

So what do we have in common? We all share a passion for space and exploration, enjoy science and try our best at everything.

Getting humans and machines into space is really difficult. Astronauts train hard so that they are ready for anything – and of course it's important to stay fit and healthy.

But it also takes brilliant scientists and engineers to design our rockets and spacesuits, and make everything work. This exciting guide will tell you a bit more about what it's like to live and work in space... and why getting there and back is such a tough job.

So, good luck on your journey and maybe I'll see you in space one day!

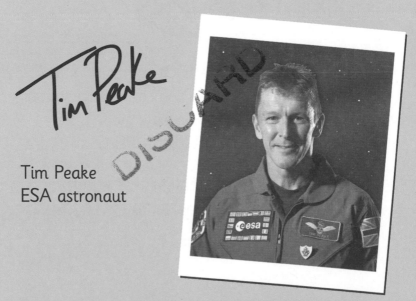

Tim Peake
ESA astronaut

Chapter One

ARE YOU CUT OUT FOR SPACE?

Want to be an astronaut? Of course you do. Who wouldn't want to float around in space, gazing back at our gorgeous blue planet, and zooming to work on a speeding rocket?

But it's tough out there. Have you got what it takes to fly in the harsh conditions of space? Or would you spend the trip terrified, screaming and shaking in a corner?

What is an astronaut?

It sounds a ridiculously easy question. An astronaut is someone who flies in space, right? Well, yes — but it's pretty difficult to say where space actually starts.

This sounds complicated. Can I just fly in a rocket now, please?

Patience, young space apprentice. (Patience is something you'll need a lot of as an astronaut.)

If you fly straight up from Earth, you'll get to space eventually. But before you do, there's a blanket of gases (the atmosphere) which gets thinner until it fades into nothing.

After that, you're in space. But the gases fade out gradually, so it's hard to say where the atmosphere ends.

Are we nearly there yet?

So what DOES count as space?

To stop disagreements, scientists have come up with a made-up line — the Karman line — 100km (62 miles) above the Earth. That's where space starts, officially speaking. Get past that line, and you're definitely an astronaut.

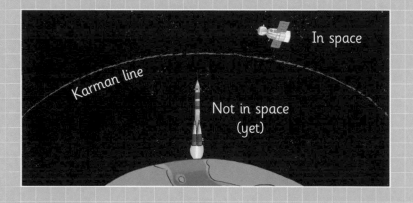

Karman line

In space

Not in space (yet)

Into space

But getting *to* the Karman line is a problem. Not many people have spaceships, as they're the most expensive form of transport known to humanity. Rolls Royces? Private jets? They're bargain basement wheelbarrows compared to your average spacecraft.

Who's paying?

To get a ride into space, you will need to do one of these things...

1. Work for a government space agency

Government space agencies are the number one employers of astronauts (and owners of spacecraft). If you're American, you could work for the National Aeronautics and Space Administration (NASA). If you live in Europe, go for the European Space Agency (ESA).

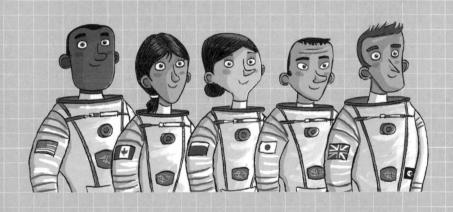

Russian? Choose Roscosmos. Japan, Canada and China have their own, too. If your country or region doesn't have an agency that hires astronauts, consider emigrating.

2. Become a billionaire

With eye-watering sums of money, you can go into space as a tourist. If that's your plan, start building your international business empire immediately.

Your spaceship's ready, Madam.

3. Work for a billionaire

If you don't end up becoming one yourself, there are at least a few billionaires who have started private space travel companies. Get a job as a pilot with one of those, and you could soon be ferrying the rich and famous into space.

4. Win a competition

Some people have won tickets into space. But none of them have flown yet, so don't hold your breath.

5. Become incredibly famous, then die...

A select few people have had their ashes blasted into space, instead of a more humdrum burial on Earth. But you'd probably rather be alive to enjoy space. All in all, your best plan is to become a professional astronaut, working for a space agency.

Here at last. Amazing!

Working for a space agency

Most professional astronauts work on a flying science lab called the International Space Station, or ISS*. There, they study everything from climate change to the effects of space on the human body (some of them unpleasant).

Where is the ISS?

The ISS is flying around and around the Earth, a few hundred miles above the planet's surface.

At the moment, astronauts don't visit other planets. This is partly because of money — it's incredibly expensive to fly far into space. But it's mostly because of our puny human bodies.

*American, Russian, Japanese, European and Canadian astronauts visit the ISS. Chinese astronauts have their own space station.

We'll need to develop technology to protect ourselves for longer missions, beyond the Moon. Fingers crossed, scientists will have invented clever solutions to the problem of human feebleness by the time you've finished your training. Then Mars missions will be all systems go.

Getting started

Before you can train as a professional astronaut you need...

✫ A degree in something like maths or engineering. (You'll need to finish school first.)

✫ To be between 157cm and 190.5cm (62-75 inches) tall. Any taller and you wouldn't fit into your spaceship. They're not the roomiest of vehicles.

Ow! I've seen tin cans with more legroom.

✡ To be a generally healthy person. Space is tough on the body, so you need to be tough too. But don't worry if you're not superhumanly fit – you won't need to be a top athlete.

✡ To be *either* an expert at flying incredibly fast jets *or* a brilliant scientist, though being both wouldn't hurt your chances.

Woo hoo! I'm hard at work. It's a tough life!

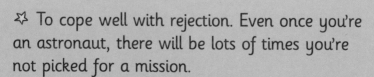

✡ To cope well with rejection. Even once you're an astronaut, there will be lots of times you're not picked for a mission.

⭐ To be ready to cheer your fellow astronauts on, not moan about them stealing 'your' place on a mission.

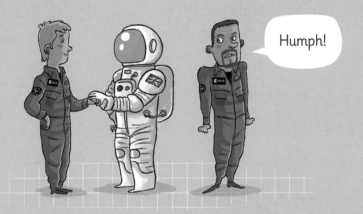

Humph!

⭐ To have no problems with confined spaces and getting along with people. If you become an astronaut, you'll spend months trapped in a metal box with other astronauts.

And that's not all. As well as meeting all these basic requirements, you have to compete with thousands of other very talented people to get a job as an astronaut.

But what if I grow too tall
to be an astronaut?

Don't despair! If you don't have exactly the right qualities to be an astronaut, but you love spaceships and space travel, there are plenty of other career options. You could be...

A mechanic or a technician – there are lots of jobs for the gadget-lover at private space companies and space agencies. Technicians operate (and fix) all kinds of machines, from laboratory computers to space robots. You might even get to drive robots on other planets.

Nobody here but
us robots.

Disclaimer: you will be doing this by remote control, via radio waves. You will not actually be racing around on Mars in a buggy yourself.

An astronaut trainer – astronauts need training in everything from how to put on a space suit to how to fly a spacecraft, so space agencies need plenty of training staff.

A flight controller – this is the person who gives astronauts their orders from Earth, sitting in a room known as 'Mission Control'. You'll need a calm head and good technical skills. The astronauts look to you for guidance, so don't take advantage of their trust.

Don't turn around. There's something in the spaceship with you. And it looks hungry.

It's your job to keep the astronauts under your command safe (and busy) – from the moment they lift off to the moment they land at the end of their mission.

A scientist or an engineer – teams of scientists and engineers work together to get spacecraft off the ground and keep them safe in space. Some design spacecraft; others do experiments to test out new materials.

Engine firing test – engineers not seen because they're standing WELL out of the way.

A flight surgeon – space agencies hire doctors to look after astronauts during their training and on missions, and to talk them through medical procedures when they're in space. If you become a flight surgeon, you'll be helping out with medical experiments in space too, so even if the crew stays perfectly healthy, you won't be twiddling your thumbs.

But if you find the idea of an Earth-bound life too frustrating, and you do meet all the requirements, then it's time to take the next steps on the road to space...

Chapter Two

CONGRATULATIONS, YOU'RE A SPACE CADET

Let's fast forward through many years of hard work. Picture yourself...

...falling asleep on a pile of homework...

...running until your lungs burst...

...learning how to fly a jet plane...

...doing even more homework.

And now, finally, at long last, you've been selected for an astronaut training programme.

This is where the hard work REALLY begins.

BASIC TRAINING

First, you'll have basic training – but don't let the word 'basic' fool you. The things you'll be learning will be very difficult indeed. That doesn't matter. You're an astronaut candidate. You do ten difficult things before breakfast.

Five 'basic' things you'll learn

1. Orbital mechanics

This is the study of how rockets and spacecraft move. Here's a typical orbital mechanics diagram.

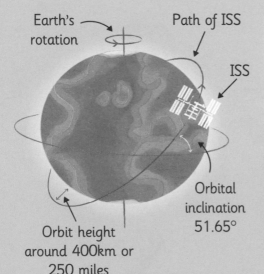

Earth's rotation

Path of ISS

ISS

Orbit height around 400km or 250 miles

Orbital inclination 51.65°

1 orbit = 92.74 minutes

How hard can it be? It's only rocket science. (Ok, technically it's rocket maths.)

2. Russian

If you're Russian, this part will be a walk in the park on a sunny day in Moscow. Otherwise, it's time to learn a whole new language – in a new alphabet.

> Why am I learning Russian?

The spacecraft used to fly up to the ISS is a Russian craft called a Soyuz. It generally helps, when you're piloting a vehicle, if you can read what it says on the buttons.

> Is that the Russian for 'on switch' or 'mission abort'?

It's also useful to know what the people at Mission Control are saying when your spaceship is about to take off, and to understand your Russian colleagues on board the ISS. (Half the crew on board are Russian.)

3. Science, engineering and robotics

You'll learn how to pilot (and fix) your Soyuz spacecraft and the ISS itself, and how to carry out scientific experiments on board. You'll also need to know how to operate robots in space.

One of the tasks you learn is how to control a robotic arm to catch a spaceship called a Dragon.

Get ready for tough courses in everything from robotics and electrical engineering to conducting scientific research in space and how to do plumbing. Someone has to fix the space toilets after all. (A broken space toilet is a serious thing.)

4. Staying alive

Training for space is about being prepared. What if your spacecraft goes off course and you land on Earth – but somewhere hostile?

Welcome home. You're just in time for dinner.

If things go wrong, you might land in the middle of an ocean, or in a frozen wasteland to the far north of nowhere-you-recognize. Earth might be home, but it's not always welcoming.

To prepare for an emergency landing, you have to complete wilderness training. You will be choppered out to a remote location, abandoned and left to fend for yourself. Remember, it's for your own good.

Hahahaha! Byeeeee!

Could you build a shelter, find food, learn to hunt and not get eaten? Your challenge begins now...

5. Surgery

In space, you and your crewmates have to be completely self-sufficient. If you feel ill, you'll only have your fellow astronauts to turn to – you can't pop to a doctor on the nearest moon.

So, if someone has a serious medical problem, guess who'll be performing emergency surgery? Why yes. It might well be you.

I need to do some amputation training. Any volunteers?

You'll be taught how to give first aid, as well as how to set a broken leg and fix lots of minor bodily troubles. (Complex surgery won't be one of the first things you'll learn, but it's on the list.)

Fingers crossed, these aren't skills you'll ever need. Even if you did, your flight surgeon back on Earth will be on the other end of a space phone to talk you through it.

Exam time (all of the time)

Your basic training will last for about a year and a half. You'll be tested regularly on everything you've learned – so no falling asleep at the back, or copying from the other astronaut candidates please.

It's not all hard study though

You'll also learn fun things like how to scuba dive. This is to prepare you for floating around in space.

Today, the training pool.
Tomorrow, the stars.

As you float around underwater, you can start to imagine what it will be like to float in space. Of course, you won't be wearing flippers there.

What will I be wearing, then?

A spacesuit – a sealed suit with a helmet and your own air supply. But you'll learn more about that as we go along. First, brace yourself... your training is about to step up a gear.

Now for the tricky tasks

Once you've completed your basic training, you're ready to move on to the really complicated stuff – such as walking, eating, and going to the toilet.

Are you serious?

You think this is a joke? Read on.

ADVANCED TRAINING

For your advanced training, you'll have to relearn all kinds of things you thought you'd mastered before you started school.

Getting dressed

In space, you have to wear a spacesuit to go outdoors, or you won't survive long. Climbing into a spacesuit is a tricky and time-consuming process involving lots of heavy pieces of equipment. You will need help.

Walking

During a mission, you might find yourself going for a walk. But this isn't ordinary walking.

You'll have to learn how to spacewalk, which is more like flying than walking. It also takes hours of preparation and safety checks before you head out of the 'door' into space.

Going to the toilet

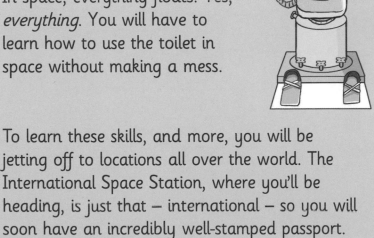

This could get complicated...

In space, everything floats. Yes, *everything*. You will have to learn how to use the toilet in space without making a mess.

To learn these skills, and more, you will be jetting off to locations all over the world. The International Space Station, where you'll be heading, is just that – international – so you will soon have an incredibly well-stamped passport.

Star City

Welcome, welcome. You are now entering Star City, in Russia, where astronauts from all over the world come to train. Star City sounds glamorous, but in reality, it's no five-star vacation resort. Prepare to experience intense discomfort and nausea. And that's just the canteen (kidding).

You can gaze upon statues of past astronauts... or rather cosmonauts as they're called in Russia.

This is Yuri Gagarin, the first person in space.

In Star City, you'll be perfecting your spacecraft-flying technique, focusing on the Russian Soyuz craft you will use to get to the ISS.

Sim City

One piece of kit you'll soon be very familiar with is the simulator. This piece of machinery is basically a computer housed inside a model spacecraft that closely resembles the inside of the one you'll be piloting.

Just like the real thing.

Yup. And just as cramped.

As you climb into the simulator's tiny interior, you will get your first sense of quite how snug a Soyuz can be.

Errors are ok

When you're in a 'sim' – or having a go in a simulator – it's your chance to make mistakes and learn from them. This means, by the time you're in space, you'll be perfect at all the moves, rather than a danger to yourself and others.

Top tip: don't accidentally turn the whole Soyuz simulation off as one cadet did.

OOPS!

In sims, you'll learn how to blast off into space, dock (join up) with another spacecraft, change direction and land. You'll spend hours staring at numbers and squiggles on computer screens. You might start to dream about them.

Despite the joysticks and flashing screens, a sim is not a computer game, it's a training tool. No alien battle noises, please. It's just not dignified.

Sim vs. space

There's one very big difference between being in the sim and being in an actual spacecraft in space. When you're working in space, you will experience something called zero-G (short for zero gravity) or microgravity.

Zero-G isn't no-G

When an astronaut floats around in space, that's zero-G at work. But zero-G doesn't actually mean 'no gravity'. It's just that, in space, you experience gravity in a different way.

Hang on, what's gravity?

Gravity is an invisible pulling force that affects us all the time. It's the reason that, in your everyday life, you don't float helplessly into the air like a lost helium balloon. It's also why you fall over when you trip, so it's not all fun and games.

What's doing the pulling?
Is it... invisible giants?

The giants guess is close. Every object has gravity – everything in the universe pulls on every other thing. But the larger the object, the bigger the pull. Giant objects have a gigantic pull.

The pull of home

The reason you don't float away on Earth is because a giant object (Earth) is pulling on a smaller object (you). If you jump up, Earth's mighty pull will bring you down again, however springy your shoes are.

What goes up must come down. Because I say so.

In turn, other planets and huge objects such as the Sun also pull strongly on Earth. The Sun's gravity affects us so much that it pulls our planet around it in circles, known as orbits. It's as if the Sun is whirling a dance partner around at thousands of miles an hour. The Sun has eight planets in orbit around it, including ours.

The Sun is boss of all the planets, thanks to its giant size – and gravity. Gravity really is everywhere. When you're in space, you're still affected by it. There is no escape.

So, if gravity's everywhere, why do astronauts float?

Excellent question. The answer is, they don't, really. It's just easier to describe it as floating than to say exactly what's happening to them.

When you're zooming around Earth in space, you and your spacecraft are moving very fast, even though it doesn't feel like it because you're going at a steady speed and there's no air whistling past you. (There is no air.)

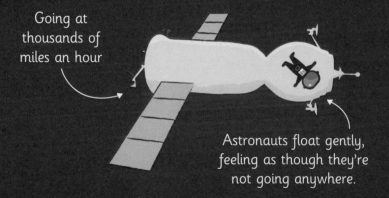

Going at thousands of miles an hour

Astronauts float gently, feeling as though they're not going anywhere.

Here's the shocker: you feel as if you're floating, but actually you're falling, and so is your spacecraft.

WHAT? AAAAARGH!

DON'T PANIC!

This isn't the kind of falling where you'll crash. Your spacecraft is moving fast enough to stop you from falling back down to Earth in a fiery ball of death.

Gravity keeps tugging at you, trying to pull you back down, but as long as you maintain the right speed, you'll keep falling around Earth rather than back down to it. That is, you'll stay in orbit.

Zero-G: when the floor's the ceiling

This falling-through-space that you experience as an astronaut is zero-G or microgravity. It's an intense and peculiar sensation. You might suddenly find your arm has floated above your head. Zero-G confuses your brain, too, making it difficult to know which way is up or down.

For the first few hours (or days) in space, this disorientation can make your lunch get confused about which way is down, too. You may get a visit from an earlier meal in your mouth.

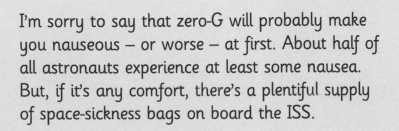

I'm sorry to say that zero-G will probably make you nauseous – or worse – at first. About half of all astronauts experience at least some nausea. But, if it's any comfort, there's a plentiful supply of space-sickness bags on board the ISS.

Don't despair — it will get better in time. But until then, don't think about greasy rotten stew and mouldy bread with an oozing worm sauce...

Sorry. Just checking to see if you have the stomach for space. Better to know now.

A little light training (and the opposite)

You'll be trained for zero-G on Earth (and above) before you ever experience it for real. At the other end of the spectrum, you'll also experience 'high-G' training, which involves feeling as though you weigh about four times as much as you usually do, and wondering whose brilliant idea it was to train to become an astronaut.

Floating in the air

For your first stint of zero-G training, you'll board a plane that's used to simulate zero-G without leaving Earth's atmosphere. (Early astronauts nicknamed a plane like this the 'Vomit Comet' but don't let that put you off.)

You'll fly up and down in steep curves known as parabolas. At the top of each parabola, you'll feel as though you're floating.

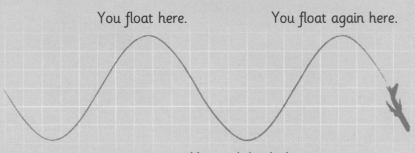

You float here.

You float again here.

You sink back down to the floor here.

It's like that moment at the top of a rollercoaster, where you're still going up while the rollercoaster car has already started going down.

But Dad I need to go again, it's part of my astronaut training.

In the plane, this 'weightless' feeling lasts for 30 seconds or so at a time. It's so much fun that you might not want to come down again.

Tip: your arms and legs won't stay where you put them. So make sure not to punch your fellow cadets accidentally.

Mind you, it could also be your first vinegary taste of space-sickness, so you might be very grateful to float back down to the ground.

Spinning around

Now it's time for high-G training, which involves being whirled around in a spinning machine called a centrifuge. Ever wondered how your clothes feel in a washing machine? You're about to find out.

As you spin, it seems as though gravity is getting stronger and stronger, pushing harder on your body. It will feel a little like this:

A spin in a centrifuge tests your ability to withstand fast acceleration in a spacecraft, as well as testing your inner ear (the part inside your head that controls balance).

How does a centrifuge work?

You must climb inside, strap yourself in, and endure being whirled around and around, faster and faster, pushed helplessly back in your seat by something known as G-forces*.

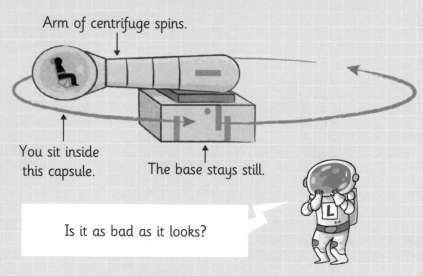

Arm of centrifuge spins.

You sit inside this capsule.

The base stays still.

Is it as bad as it looks?

Worse. Prepare to feel very squashed indeed. You might even pass out. This is known as G-LOC which stands for 'G-force induced loss of consciousness'. (If you turn something into a string of letters, it sounds like a secret code, not a terrifying and deeply uncomfortable experience.)

*The G stands for gravity. It feels as though it should stand for gaaaaaaahhhh!

I'm S.C.A.R.E.D.

Try not to worry. Painfully high G-forces are only likely on a mission if something goes very wrong. On average, space launches and landings exert similar G-forces on your body to racing cars, fighter jets and rollercoasters.

A trip to the pool

Your zero-G training continues underwater, in a 'neutral buoyancy environment'. Or, as most people would call it, a swimming pool. Still, it's not just any swimming pool. This one has spaceships at the bottom.

Underwater D.I.Y.

When you float around in this very special swimming pool, with help from divers, you'll get a sense of what it's like to work while you're weightless. Your spacesuit will be tweaked to suit the underwater work, but it's as close as you can get to the experience of being in space without leaving the ground.

Life-size copies of parts of the ISS are installed at the bottom of the pool.

The pool gives you the opportunity to try out all the tasks you will have to perform when you're outside in space, from operating a drill to checking on a science experiment.

Chosen at last

And now, at long last, the moment you've been waiting for. You have been selected to fly on a mission to the ISS.

But remember the comment about patience at the start of the book? You now have about two more years of training. There's so much still to do...

It's time for the catchily-named:

MISSION-SPECIFIC TRAINING

This will vary depending on which mission you've been assigned. But it's your opportunity to bond with the two other people who'll be on your Soyuz crew. You'll have to learn to work together as a team — you'll depend on each other for everything once you're in space.

Warning: as the members of your team get to know one another and start to feel relaxed, you are highly likely to be a victim of pranks.

After so much hard work, everyone needs to blow off a little steam. So don't be surprised if you come back exhausted from training to find someone's glued your toothbrush to its holder or replaced your bed with an inflatable hippo.

What will training be like?

Dry runs for EVERYTHING

Every moment that you spend in space is precious – in the precious sparkling diamonds sense. It costs a lot to keep an astronaut up there and there's no time to get things wrong.

That's why you will have to perform dry runs (or, in some cases, wet runs in the pool) of every single task that you'll do on your mission – even things that seem ridiculously simple.

Lunch training isn't so bad.

Scientific experiments

A lot of your time on board the ISS is spent doing scientific experiments. During your mission-specific training, you will be going over and over (and over and over) these until you feel as if you might turn into a test tube.

Planning for emergencies

Being prepared for all the things that might go wrong in space is very important. That means you'll learn how to keep a calm head in a stressful situation and solve any possible problem you might encounter.

Asteroid heading my way? No problem. I have a plan for that.

In training, you go through all the worst case scenarios so that you can cope with whatever space throws at you.

Still, however many precautions you take, space travel is very risky. But if you spent your life avoiding risks, you'd never do anything. Driving in a car is risky, but many people do it every day.

Photography

There are no professional photographers on the ISS, so you need to learn how to take stunning photos of Earth to delight those below.

Earth, are you ready for your close-up?

Learning how to give interviews

People will be queuing up to interview you about going into space. As part of your training, you'll be taught how to talk to reporters without saying too many silly things. One tip: check if you have spinach in your teeth or toothpaste on your face before going on TV.

Exercising

You will need to be fit and healthy to cope with the demands of your mission. Space is tough on your body — especially on your bones and muscles. Exercising a lot before you go will make life easier for you in the long run. (And some of your runs will feel very long indeed.)

Endless health checks

To make sure that you're healthy enough to fly, you'll be poked, prodded, pulled, pushed and generally pestered.

Scientists will cluster around you to do experiments on your body, too. When you get into space, you won't get a break from this. A lot of the time, you ARE the experiment.

Whatever you do, don't catch something in the days before the mission – or you'll be thrown off and have to wait for a new assignment.

So stay away from people with runny noses and make sure to eat plenty of fruit and veg. Also, don't go skiing or do other dangerous sports. Unsurprisingly, they won't let you fly into space with your leg in a cast.

Wait...

Launch day might seem a long way off. But you will get there – eventually. Most of the time you'll be so busy training, getting fitted for spacesuits, giving interviews and brushing up your language skills that the weeks will just fly by.

Chapter Three
LIFTOFF

Fantastic news! Liftoff day's in sight and very soon you'll be an astronaut. Before you go, you'll need to be fitted for a suit to wear while you're blasted into orbit. Just as on Earth, you need the right outfit for each activity.

Suit up

For takeoff and landing in a Soyuz spacecraft, you'll wear a protective suit called a 'Sokol' suit.

Your helmet has a microphone so you can talk to Mission Control.

This blue seal on the chest keeps all the air inside — and you alive.

These tubes link up to an oyxgen supply in the Soyuz so you can breathe in an emergency.

A Sokol suit is designed to protect you in case something goes wrong on the way up or the way down from space.

But on its own, it's not enough to protect you.

Bottoms up!

In order to keep you from being bounced around during liftoff and landing you get your own chair lining in your Soyuz seat. This has to be shaped to fit your rear end while you lie with your legs in the air like a baby being changed.

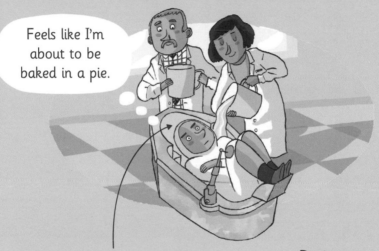

Feels like I'm about to be baked in a pie.

A substance called gypsum is poured around you. It sets to create a you-shaped outline.

Don't worry. You won't get stuck as it sets.

This made-to-measure seat lining helps to keep you snug and safe. What you lose in dignity now, you'll gain in not getting shaken to death when you're riding a rocket into space and back.

Launch day

So, you have your own
suit, you've been fitted for
your chair... it's time. You're
going to space. You're
going to space TODAY.
Are you excited? Are you
jumping up and down?

Well, stop that.

You're supposed to be cool, calm and
professional, at least on the outside. The world's
media will be watching. On the inside, however,
feel free to burst – almost – with the thrill of the
fact that, in a few hours, you will be in space.

In the middle of nowhere

Before launch, you'll arrive at Baikonur
Cosmodrome – one of Earth's main spaceports,
in a particularly empty part of Kazakhstan, a
country to the south of Russia. (Don't be fooled
by the 'south' part. It's still freezing for a lot of
the year.)

You'll receive a hero's welcome and pose for
many, many photos.

You'll sign lots of autographs...
you'll even sign doors.

It's traditional for crews to sign the bedroom
doors at the Cosmonaut Hotel – the posher-than-
it-sounds building where astronauts stay the night
before they launch. This 'hotel' has been used by
hundreds of astronauts, so it might be a struggle
to find room for your signature.

Counting down

The time before launch is measured backwards.
When you hear someone talking about *T minus
5 hours*, that means five hours before liftoff.
(Once people start talking about *T plus...* you've
missed your flight.)

Time to suit up

At about T minus 3 hours, it's time to get dressed. When you're in your Sokol suit, ground crew will buzz around you checking, checking and checking again that everything is in working order.

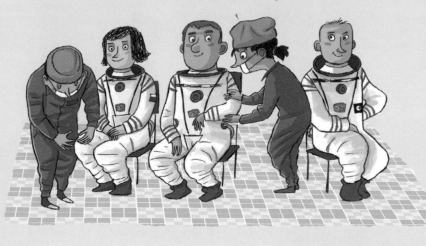

Why are they wearing masks?

This is to stop them sneezing on you, or otherwise spreading their germs. Getting ill on the ISS would make your mission utterly miserable so, before launch, you'll be kept apart from other people except for fellow crew members, or very-carefully-scrubbed people wearing masks.

Fish bowl astronauts

The world's media will be desperate to speak to you. To do this without catching germs, you'll face them through a glass wall and talk into a microphone. If anyone asks any awkward questions, you could always fake a technical hitch.

Krrrrsk....krsssk....sorry I can't....krrrsk hear you.

Urine Gagarin

People always tell you to go to the toilet before a long journey. The same is true for space travel. But at Baikonur Cosmodrome you might end up doing so very publicly.

The first human in space, Yuri Gagarin, was caught short before liftoff and had to go next to the truck that carried him to the launch pad. It's become traditional to do the same.

Expect the bus to make a stop before you reach the launch pad so you can follow in Yuri's footsteps. (Watch where you put your feet.)

Into the rocket

Finally, you'll walk to the rocket, surrounded by ground crew, side-by-side with your crewmates. This is your moment.

You reach your majestic rocket. Look up and drink in all 49.5m (162 feet, 5 inches) of it. It's surrounded by what looks like scaffolding. This is known as the launch tower. It's not going to space with you; it will pull back just before launch, to set you free. Don't worry about the climb, either: there's a lift.

The Soyuz spacecraft that will be your taxi nestles inside the nose cone of the rocket.

If the Soyuz is a spacecraft, why can't it just fly into space on its own?

A spacecraft, such as a Soyuz, is designed to fly *in* space. But to get into space in the first place, you need a launch vehicle, or rocket. A rocket is basically a collection of engines used to overcome Earth's gravity and push upwards into space.

Most of a rocket is hollow and full of fuel. The rest is made up of engines to burn that fuel and force it out of the bottom, pushing the rocket upwards.

Rockets are usually made up of different parts, known as stages. Each stage contains its own store of fuel, plus an engine.

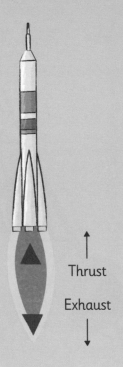

Thrust

Exhaust

The exhaust pushes down. This creates an upwards push called thrust.

So, I'm launching into space on a jet of fire. Is this really a good idea?

You're right to be a little cautious. Rocket fuel is very, very flammable, and if a rocket went wrong, it could explode. This is where the ground support crews are vital. They will check every last inch of your rocket and spacecraft, to make sure nothing's leaking or loose. You're in good hands.

Welcome to your ship

After taking the lift up to the top of the rocket, you and your two crewmates will climb in through a hatch in the 'orbital module' of your Soyuz spacecraft. Then you'll clamber through the cramped interior until you reach the 'crew module', which is where you sit for liftoff.

This is what your spacecraft looks like when it's not stuffed inside a rocket.

Orbital module *aka* the living room of the spacecraft – where you sit (or rather float) for a while once you're in space but before you reach the ISS.

Crew module – where you'll sit during launch and landing. Very, very cramped.

Propulsion module – where the engine is, plus supplies of oxygen and other gear.

Know your place

Once you're in the crew module, you'll take your seat. Which seat depends on your job on this mission.

If you're the commander in charge of the mission, you'll take the middle seat.

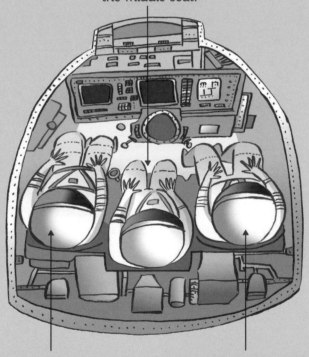

If you're the flight engineer, take the seat to the commander's left.

This seat is either for a second flight engineer or, very occasionally, a flight participant (such as a billionaire space tourist).

Note: the middle seat is a little further back than the others, so the commander has to press the controls using a stick. (Nothing but the most hi-tech tech on board the Soyuz.)

Sit (very, very) tight

You'll be strapped in here for about two hours while the nice people at Mission Control run checks on your spacecraft. I have to be honest with you, the accommodation is not spacious. If you had a cat, you couldn't swing it. In fact, the cat wouldn't be able to swing a mouse. 'Get comfortable' would be a cruel thing to say at this point.

On the plus side, you'll be able to listen to music. And remember: better to spend two hours with your knees shoved up against your chest than for a loose bolt on the rocket to cause an accident.

This is it... this... is... it!

The hatch is closed, the ground team's checks are complete, the countdown gets to zero and the huge rocket engine starts to fire. You don't need to do anything at this point — it's all automatic, just like a washing machine cycle (only with fire). All you need to do is keep an eye on the screens and check that everything is going smoothly. Are you ready? Three... two... one...

LIFTOFF!

Wait a minute

Liftoff happens quite slowly at first. So, let's take a moment. There's something important that we should probably talk about. In a few minutes' time, your beautiful rocket will be in pieces, plummeting back towards the Earth.

What? HELP!

Sorry, was that a little too dramatic? You can relax. The rockets that launch spacecraft are designed to fall off once the fuel has been used up. That way, your spacecraft doesn't have to carry any useless weight, making it easier to beat Earth's gravity and lift off into space.

By the time you're in space, all the parts on the outside will have dropped off...

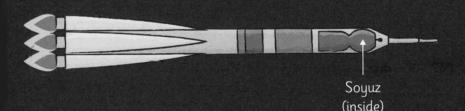

Soyuz
(inside)

Only the bold little Soyuz will remain, flying free in space. (With you and your crew safely inside it, in case you're still worried.)

How your rocket works (and how it falls apart)

Just after liftoff, your rocket looks like this. All the engines at the bottom are firing.

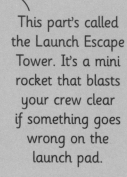

This part's called the Launch Escape Tower. It's a mini rocket that blasts your crew clear if something goes wrong on the launch pad.

Four rockets known as boosters are the first to use up their fuel and come off. That's the first rocket stage over and done with.

Once you're in the air, the escape tower comes off.

Bye bye, boosters!

Watch out below! The boosters may be out of fuel, but they still weigh roughly the same as an elephant... each.

Boosters

Soon it's time to lose the second stage and the nose cone (a protective case around the Soyuz). The third stage starts its engines.

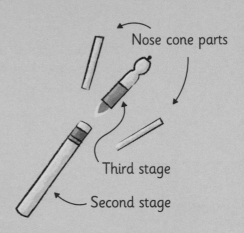

Nose cone parts

Third stage

Second stage

Finally, the third stage falls off and your Soyuz is flying solo. The solar panels you'll use for power spread out like wings.

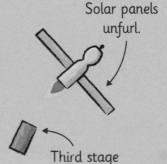

Solar panels unfurl.

Third stage

What happens to the parts that fall off?

The first two stages and other no-longer-needed parts fall back down to Earth with a massive bump, in (everyone hopes) a deserted part of Kazakhstan. The third stage burns up in a ball of fire like a metal meteor.

Ok, so that's what happens to the rocket... but what does liftoff feel like from inside the Soyuz?

In a word: thrilling. Everything is shaking. From the muffled roar, you might imagine you're sitting on the shoulders of a slowly waking and very grumpy giant.

Your eyes are glued to the computer screens in front of you, full of information about your rocket's performance – how fast it's going, how much fuel it's using. Thanks to your hours of training, you know exactly what all the information means.

You lift off from the ground, ever so slowly at first. Fingers crossed, you'll hear this from Mission Control...

Everything is nominal*.

PHEW!

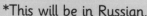
*This will be in Russian.

Nominal means 'everything's going as expected'. This is a good thing. Remember: surprises are bad in space travel.

Then you start to build up speed, and gravity presses you back down into your seat. But if all goes well, you won't experience anything like the G-forces you had in training. It'll feel more like a couple of your mates piling onto your lap (and your chest, and your arms and legs, and your face). Then there's a massive...

But it's a nominal* sort of a bang. That's just part of the rocket separating – the escape tower – which you don't need since everything's fine.

*If you've already forgotten what this means, you might want to do some memory-training exercises before you apply to be an astronaut...

You'll hear a few of these bangs. This is nothing to worry about. It's just the sound of each rocket stage dropping off once it's used up all its fuel. Remember: this is part of the design. Rockets are meant to come apart.

KLANG

Cue more noises and jolts, and a breathless feeling in your chest as gravity slams you down against your seat. The minutes pass until...

KERBANG!

The final rocket engine separates. Something strange happens soon after that...

A little toy hanging from the roof of your cockpit starts to rise up into the air. (Every space launch has one of these. They're usually chosen by the commander's children, so it will probably be something cute and/or fluffy.)

Do you feel strange? Arms floating in front of you? You are now experiencing zero-G. You're also past the Karman line.

Which means... drumroll... you are in space.

Yipeee!

Congratulations! You're officially an astronaut!

Chapter Four

YOUR NEW HOME

Now you're in space, you need to join up with the International Space Station, which will be your home, office and, in fact, your entire world for the next six months or so.

Joining up two spacecraft is known as docking, and it's a very tricky process: imagine trying to park a car when the parking spot is moving at thousands of miles an hour, and so are you.

Docking instructions

1. Get into the same orbit as the ISS. You'll need to be about 400km (250 miles) above Earth.

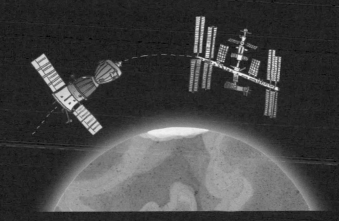

2. Make sure you're not flying too quickly, so that you don't smash into the station as you move closer.

3. Catch up (carefully) with the space station and line up the nose of your Soyuz with one of the empty docking spots (known as ports) on the ISS.

4. Slip the pointed part at the front of your Soyuz into a dip in one of the docking ports on the outside of the ISS and wait to hear a satisfying clunk. You're locked on tight!

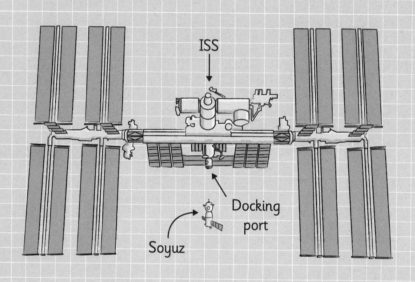

ISS

Docking port

Soyuz

Note: most of this should happen automatically, but you need to keep your eyes peeled and your button-pressing fingers (or sticks) at the ready in case anything goes wrong.

When Mission Control says that everything is ready, it's time to open the hatch and float through into the ISS.

After the cramped Soyuz, you can finally have a proper stretch. What a relief!

Welcome... now call your mother

The crew already on the station will be very excited to see you and your crew. You're the only new faces they've seen in months that aren't on a TV screen. Expect hugging.

Next, you'll have a quick safety tour and then a chat with your family back on Earth. Most of the time on board the ISS, you'll get to chat with your family in private, but this one will be streamed live on the internet.

So perhaps don't air any family secrets.

By the time you've done all that, you might need to visit the littlest room on the spaceship.

Space toilets suck

When you relieve yourself on Earth, gravity makes sure that everything goes down the toilet bowl. In zero-G, the toilet uses suction (like a vacuum cleaner) to make sure nothing ends up floating free.

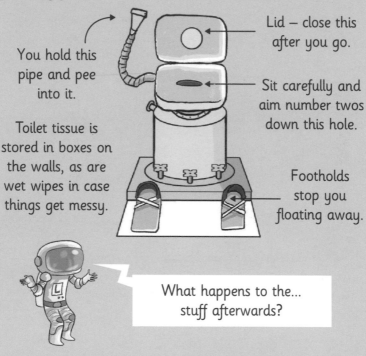

You hold this pipe and pee into it.

Toilet tissue is stored in boxes on the walls, as are wet wipes in case things get messy.

Lid – close this after you go.

Sit carefully and aim number twos down this hole.

Footholds stop you floating away.

What happens to the... stuff afterwards?

Urine is recycled into drinking water. If you think that's disgusting, it's what happens on Earth, too. At least in space you know exactly whose recycled fluids you're drinking, as there are only a few people on board. (Six, usually.)

> What happens to the... solid stuff?

It's gathered in bags and stored, along with other refuse. Later, it's packed into a type of uncrewed spacecraft, called a Progress, that carries supplies to the ISS.

As each Progress craft heads back towards Earth, it carries those packages of waste. But the ship doesn't make it home. It burns up in a ball of flames when it hits Earth's atmosphere.

> Is that a shooting star?

> No, it's astronaut poo.

Your stomach in space

As you learned during your training, strange things happen to your stomach in space. NASA very politely calls this 'stomach awareness'. You might prefer to call it 'feeling as though you're going to heave your insides out through your gulping throat'.

Unless you're incredibly unlucky, however, your body will adjust over time and you'll feel better.

When your stomach is up to it, you should eat something. All the crew usually gather together at mealtimes, like a family, only with less squabbling.

Playing with your food is ok, as long as you don't lose it. A rotten banana floating through the station is no fun for anyone.

Velcro to keep things in place

Packet of dried eggs. Add hot water to eat.

Waste bag

Scissors to cut open sealed food bags. Be extra careful where these float.

Drink bag

Eating in zero-G takes some getting used to, as food can easily escape and float away, so take your lead from the people who've been on the station for a while.

Your menu will be varied but a lot of the food is dried, as there's no refrigerator, and fresh fruit and veg are only delivered every few months. You might want to add a lot of chilli sauce to your food, too, as zero-G dampens your taste buds.

Hot chilli sauce

On Earth, fluids such as snot drain down, thanks to gravity. But in space, they pool, making you stuffed up, so only very strong tastes will make an impact. Chilli sauce is your friend on the ISS.

Get some rest

When dinner's all cleaned up, it's time for bed. You'll be sleeping in a bag, hooked onto a wall (or a floor, or a ceiling) so you don't float away. Sleep tight!

Zzzzzzz

Chapter Five
LET'S GET TO WORK

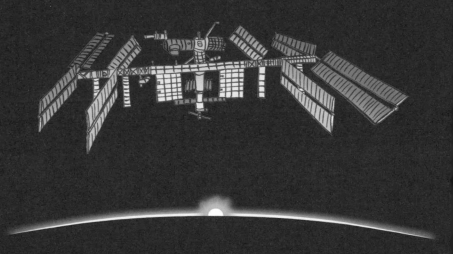

Rise and shine, a new day has dawned. Several,
actually – the ISS makes about 16 orbits of
Earth in 24 hours, which means the Sun 'rises'
and 'sets' past your portholes 16 times for every
sunrise and sunset you'd see on Earth. So you'll
sleep through plenty of 'days' in space.

While you're awake, you'll pack in a lot, and your schedules are always carefully worked out by a team at Mission Control. For example...

06:00 - Wake up, wash, eat and read emails.

07:30 - Morning meeting, where you'll discuss your schedule for the day.

08:15 - Exercise time, for about two hours. (More on this later.) Wash the sweat off.

11:00 - Check on one of the station's many science experiments.

13:00 - Lunch. (Don't forget to add chilli sauce.)

14:00 - Time for an interview over Skype with some schoolchildren. They will probably ask you how you poo in space. Almost everyone does.

15:30 - One of your colleagues is going on a spacewalk tomorrow and it's your turn to help them prepare their spacesuit. (If you're lucky, it'll be your turn for a spacewalk next time.)

19:30 - Dinner, then free time to send emails, play the guitar, watch a movie, look at how pretty Earth is.

21:30 - Bedtime. Zzzzzzz...

A plan of the office

Your new office (and home) is made up of sections, known as modules, and it's massive, so you can enjoy the feeling of stretching out and flying* through it like a superhero.

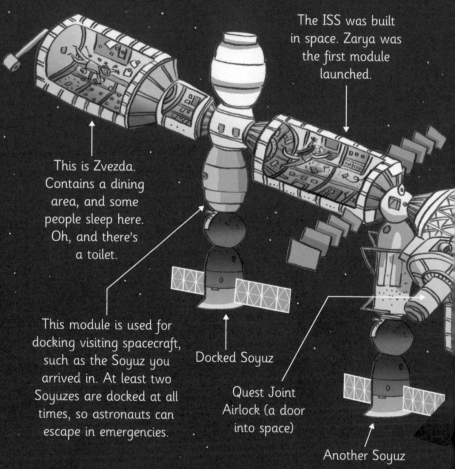

The ISS was built in space. Zarya was the first module launched.

This is Zvezda. Contains a dining area, and some people sleep here. Oh, and there's a toilet.

This module is used for docking visiting spacecraft, such as the Soyuz you arrived in. At least two Soyuzes are docked at all times, so astronauts can escape in emergencies.

Docked Soyuz

Quest Joint Airlock (a door into space)

Another Soyuz

* Reminder: you're falling, technically, but don't let that get in the way of your superhero impressions.

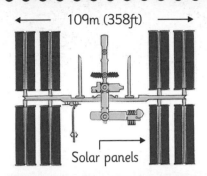

← 109m (358ft) →

Solar panels

This is what the ISS looks like from above. The map below doesn't show the solar panels structure, because it's gigantic.

There's a spectacular window into space called the Cupola. Take pics here.

This area is used to store scientific experiments.

This is where the solar panels attach.

The Japanese labs are here.

This lab is run by NASA. It's called Destiny.

Columbus is a European laboratory module.

Now you know your way around, it's time to go to work. Are you ready?

Let's make some science happen

Your most important job on board the ISS is to carry out science experiments. Astronauts on board spend a lot of each day studying what zero-G conditions do to people and objects.

This will help astronauts of the future to travel further into space. Think of these experiments as homework for going to Mars.

Playing with fire

In NASA's Destiny laboratory, you'll find a strange see-through box with a pair of gloves shoved in through two holes. This is the Microgravity Science Glovebox (MSG).

The MSG keeps scientific samples safe and stops experiments from floating off. Some of the glovebox experiments involve fire. This is known as combustion science, which is a posh way of saying 'setting fire to stuff to see what happens'. You'll find fire burns very differently in zero-G...

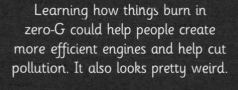

Learning how things burn in zero-G could help people create more efficient engines and help cut pollution. It also looks pretty weird.

Candle flame on Earth

Candle flame in zero-G

Every mission is different, so you can't predict what you, personally, will be studying. To give you an idea of the types of experiments that might be in store, here are a few that have already been done, or at least started...

Getting sweaty

One astronaut has tested different types of clothing, to see which ones are better at carrying sweat away from the body in zero-G.

Making spare parts

On board, you'll find a machine called a 3-D printer. It heats plastic and squirts it into shapes, building up objects, layer by layer, like this:

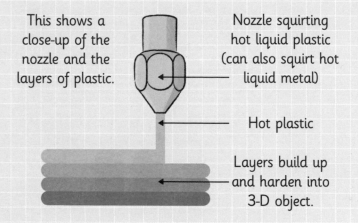

This shows a close-up of the nozzle and the layers of plastic.

Nozzle squirting hot liquid plastic (can also squirt hot liquid metal)

Hot plastic

Layers build up and harden into 3-D object.

The 3-D printer is housed inside the MSG and astronauts are taking it for a zero-G test drive. The idea is that, in the future, people will be able to use it to create spare parts for spaceships – very useful on deep-space missions, when popping to Earth for new parts won't be possible.

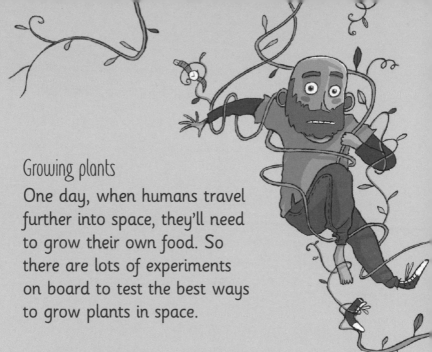

Growing plants

One day, when humans travel further into space, they'll need to grow their own food. So there are lots of experiments on board to test the best ways to grow plants in space.

Growing foot fungus

There's an infection that grows between human toes called athlete's foot. Astronauts on the ISS have brought up samples with them to study how it grows. (The samples are kept in the lab, not between the astronauts' toes.)

Making your life easier

There are usually six astronauts at a time on the ISS. But there's another astronaut-shaped crew member, a robot known as Robonaut 2. It can either be operated by an astronaut on board, or remotely from Mission Control.

Robonaut 2 can be operated using special movement-sensitive gloves and a visor that allows you to see what the robot's cameras can see. In this case, the floor.

At the moment, Robonaut 2 is being taught how to do simple tasks. The idea is that, in the long run, it will be able to take over the more boring or dangerous tasks from the crew, so astronauts can do more of the fun jobs.

Donating your body to science
(You get it back afterwards)

In a lot of the scientific studies on board, YOU are the experiment. Astronauts test how their bodies work in space, by wearing heart monitors and testing their own reactions and abilities. These tests are vital for the future of space travel, as well as teaching us more about the human body.

Erm, what kind of tests?

It *could* be something invasive and unpleasant, but might be as simple as an eye test. Astronauts have discovered that your eyesight gets worse in space. It's not too bad on an ISS trip, but explorers going further could run into big trouble.

This looks like a good planet to explore.

DANGER: KILLER SPACE BEES

Killer radiation

The Sun is a lovely thing. It makes life on Earth possible, giving us heat and light. But it also throws out dangerous radiation – invisible energy that can do nasty things to your body.

On Earth, you're protected from this by the atmosphere and by Earth's magnetic field – an invisible shield created by the planet's magnetic metal core.

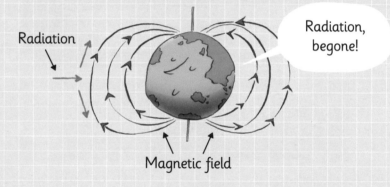

Radiation

Radiation, begone!

Magnetic field

In space, astronauts have no protection from the atmosphere. They're still protected by Earth's magnetic field, but less so than people on the planet. The further you go into space, the more exposed you are.

ISS astronauts are testing how much radiation they get exposed to on board. Scientists will have to develop better ways of shielding ships if we want to explore deep space and come back alive.

Crumbling bones

Because you're not experiencing the same pull of gravity as on Earth, your bones get weaker and lighter. Floating may be fun, but it's very bad for you. (Like many fun things.)

Bone loss is partly solved by exercises that put pressure on your bones, which is what usually happens to them in Earth's gravity.

On board the ISS, astronauts are experimenting with different types of exercises, as well as eating different types of food, to work out the best ways to protect your skeleton.

This is an exercise machine on board the ISS called the Advanced Resistive Exercise Device.

Hurrgh! I hope my skeleton says thanks later.

Screen suggests personalised exercises.

Pistons create resistance, making you work hard. Very hard.

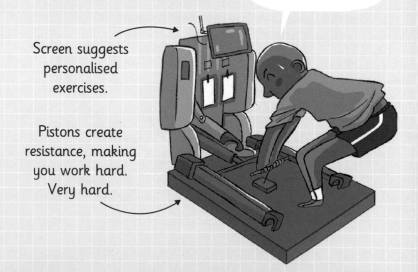

Weedy muscles

Like your bones, your muscles suffer in space. This can be really dangerous. Your heart is a muscle too, and if it shrinks too much, it might stop working.

Will that happen to me on the ISS?

It's not a problem on a trip of a year or so, but it might be on a longer voyage. Getting to Jupiter and then having a heart attack would be disappointing to say the least.

Even though you won't die if you don't exercise on the ISS, you will need to exercise for several hours every day if you want to be able to walk when you get home.

Wobble wobble

While you do your regulation two hours of exercise each day, you won't get bored. You can watch films as you work out. Also, you can enjoy the novelty of exercising on the 'ceiling', while someone else does experiments on the 'floor'. 'Up' and 'down'? Bah, those are for puny Earthlings.

Washing

After all that exercise you might be in need of a wash. Water's too precious for you to have a proper long, hot shower – not to mention the fact that zero-G makes water go everywhere – so you'll have to make do with wiping dirt and sweat from your skin, and squirting water and shampoo very, very carefully onto your hair to wash it.

Suited to spacewalks

If you get the chance to go for a spacewalk, you'll need serious protection. The type of spacesuit used on a spacewalk is often known as an Extra Vehicular Activity, or EVA, suit.

Why do I need protection?

Exposure to space would leave you unconscious in twelve seconds... and dead in about two minutes. Think of your spacesuit as your personal, miniature spaceship.

EVA suits protect you from...

Radiation damage – even though Earth's magnetic field gives you some protection when you're on a spacewalk outside the ISS, space radiation is still dangerous, so your suit has many layers to protect you from it.

Suffocation – there's no air in space, so your suit keeps you supplied with oxygen.

Extreme temperatures – it can get both blisteringly hot and blood-freezingly cold in space, depending on whether you're facing the Sun or in the shade.

Swelling up like a balloon – strangely enough, no one has volunteered to do a test of what would happen to your body if you stepped out into space in your normal clothes. But your body would probably swell up due to the lack of air pressure. To stop this, your suit is pumped full of air that pushes on your body, just as the air on Earth does.

EVA suits don't protect you from you

Unfortunately, a spacesuit does not protect you from your own body. So, if you fart, you're stuck with the smell until your spacewalk is over. (Spacewalks usually last for hours.)

The EMU

The type of suit you'll wear depends on what country you're from. First up, the Extravehicular Mobility Unit... or EMU, for short.

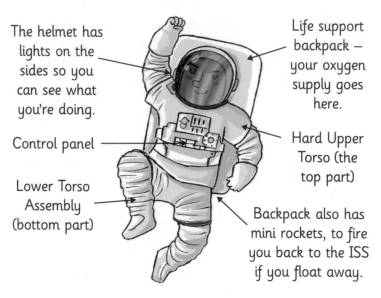

The helmet has lights on the sides so you can see what you're doing.

Control panel

Lower Torso Assembly (bottom part)

Life support backpack – your oxygen supply goes here.

Hard Upper Torso (the top part)

Backpack also has mini rockets, to fire you back to the ISS if you float away.

This is worn by American, European, Canadian and Japanese astronauts.

Learn to share

As EMU suits cost millions each, you won't get your own. But the suits are made up of lots of separate parts, so you can mix and match to get the perfect fit. An EMU goes on piece by piece, like a jigsaw puzzle with you in the middle.

1. First, you put on your astronaut underwear.

2. Then you put on the Lower Torso Assembly.

Liquid Cooling Garment

(It's not actually made of liquid. Little pipes in the outfit carry liquid around to keep you cool.)

3. Next, you wriggle into the Hard Upper Torso, from below. It's like diving into a pool only diving up.

4. Finally, you add the communications cap, gloves and helmet.

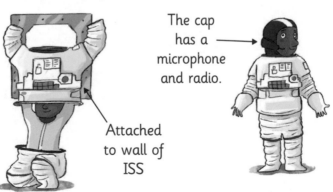

The cap has a microphone and radio.

Attached to wall of ISS

You'll need help getting dressed from your fellow astronauts, as EMUs are not very bendy, and you won't be able to reach parts of yourself once you're in the suit.

It's like the olden days, when knights needed help from squires to put on their breastplates and gauntlets and so on. Only instead of riding into battle you will be soaring into space.

My suit weighs more than yours on Earth. But in zero-G, it feels light as a feather.

Verily, thou hast all the luck.

Erm, how do I go to the toilet when I'm wearing a spacesuit?

There's no delicate way of saying this. You will have to wear a nappy underneath everything, and if you need to go while you're on a spacewalk, you'll have to use it. But, like most space equipment, your underwear has a jumble-of-letters code name, so it's less embarrassing.

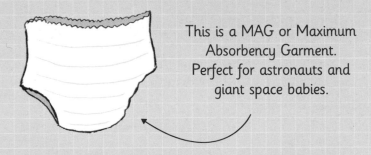

This is a MAG or Maximum Absorbency Garment. Perfect for astronauts and giant space babies.

Russian Orlan

If you're Russian, the EMU is not for you. The spacesuit worn by Russian cosmonauts is known as the Orlan. Fashions don't change very often in spacesuits. If you met a cosmonaut time tourist from 1977, you'd realize that your outfits were almost matching.

The word Orlan means 'sea eagle' in Russian. That makes it sound more graceful than you'll feel climbing inside.

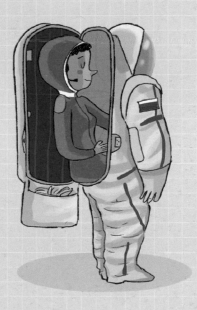

The Orlan spacesuit is a little easier to put on than an EMU, although you'll still need help. It comes in one piece and you climb in through the back.

Working in the great outdoors

Are you ready to go outside? It could be the most amazing and life-changing experience you will ever have.

Going outside in space and seeing Earth hanging there often gives astronauts a profound sense of how precious our planet is. If you ever needed a motivation to recycle more and pollute less, this will be it.

It's so beautiful.

If you cry in space, your tears will pool in floating blobs, so crying is best avoided.

Getting ready

But before you experience the beauty of Earth from space, there's a lot of preparation to do. When going on an EVA (Extra Vehicular Activity, *aka* a spacewalk) you can't just pop open a porthole and float out into the black.

How DO I get outside, then?

Very, very slowly, using a two-part space door called an airlock. Here's how it works...

1. You float into the Equipment Lock, where you:

· put on your spacesuit.
· spend 50 minutes breathing pure oxygen and doing exercises.*
· check you put your suit on properly. And check again.

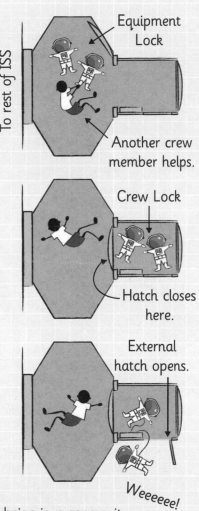

Equipment Lock

To rest of ISS

Another crew member helps.

2. Float into the second part of the airlock — the Crew Lock. An airtight hatch seals you in. Check your suit again.

Crew Lock

Hatch closes here.

3. The air is pumped out of the Crew Lock so it matches the airlessness of space. When that's done, you open the hatch leading into space and float outside.

External hatch opens.

Weeeeee!

*This helps your body adapt to being in a spacesuit and can prevent a nasty illness called 'the Bends'.

Now, before you do anything else, connect your tether – a cord that you hook on to both your suit and the outside of the spacecraft. Otherwise you could float off into space. Tether attached? Then it's time to drink in the view.

Can you fix it?

When you can tear your eyes away from Earth, it's time to get to work. One vital job is doing repairs to the outside of the station. Keeping everything running smoothly is essential. This ship is what keeps you and your crew alive after all.

Fingers and thumbs

By now you should be used to microgravity. But working inside a spacesuit has its own challenges. Your huge gloves make any fiddly tasks almost impossible. Luckily, you'll have specially designed tools, like this one below, that are simple to operate.

Like you, your stuff needs tethers too. You'll be wearing a tool belt with lots of tethers on it. You can also clip tools to loops on the outside of the station.

It might look like a space blaster, but it's actually a Pistol Grip Tool, a multi-purpose space drill.

Every now and then, astronauts do drop things — especially tiny things such as nuts and bolts. Humans have left quite a lot in orbit, from dropped gloves to broken old spacecraft. This is known as 'space junk' and there are thousands of pieces of it whizzing around out there.

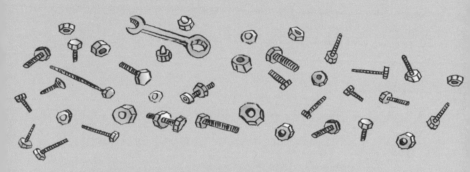

Nuts, bolts, gloves and other lost objects could potentially damage the space station if there's a collision. Please don't drop anything, as you'd be adding to the problem.

Mission Control, I have a confession to make...

Coming back inside

When you've finished your work — it might be fixing a camera on the outside of the ISS, installing a solar panel, or just checking that nothing has been damaged when some debris hit — it's time to come inside. Just as on the way out, this is a slow process, with lots and lots of safety checks. You can't be too careful in space.

Aaaaand... relax

A spacewalk is very physically draining — it can take up to eight hours, and you don't generally get to eat during that time. So when you're back inside, you'll need to eat and rest.

Everyone has their own spot on board, where they sleep, and store personal things, such as photographs of family and friends.

Miss you, boy.

In your time off in the evenings, or at weekends, you can catch up on your hobbies – whether that's watching movies, playing a musical instrument, making quilts or anything else you enjoy. (Unless your hobby requires gravity – trampolining is not an option.) Some astronauts even do extra science experiments for fun.

Space celebrity

You'll probably do a lot of video interviews, with everyone from children to world leaders, while you're up there. It's fine to enjoy the attention, but try to be modest, all the same. No one likes a space showoff.

When you're not talking to VIPs and young fans, you can call home, too. You know how parents worry.

How's your health?

Carefully monitored using advanced scientific equipment, thanks, Dad!

Chapter Six

DOWN WITH A BUMP

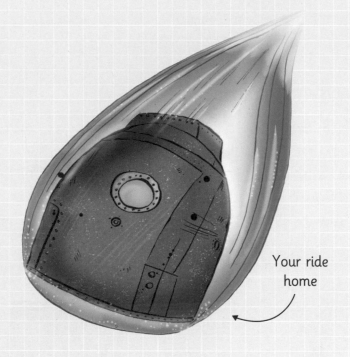

Your ride
home

All good things must come to an end. At the end of your mission — which might be six months long, or even a year — it will be time to come back down to Earth. And there will be an almighty, spine-jarring bump when you do...

Goodbye station!

In the days before you leave, you'll have to warm up the Soyuz, checking it's all in working order. Then you pack your things, plus samples from scientific experiments to be studied on Earth.

One crew brought back some flies that had been born in space as part of a study.

Hi, I'm Buzzzzzz Aldrin*.

It might be hard to believe you're leaving. But once you climb back into your Sokol suit, the reality hits you: you're going home. You hug your colleagues who are staying behind, give the station one last, longing look, and float through into the Soyuz.

You're back in your teeny-tiny space taxi once again. Time to close the hatch and prepare to depart.

*Buzz Aldrin was one of the first astronauts to walk on the Moon. He is not, in fact, a fly.

When Mission Control gives the signal, your Soyuz unhooks itself from the station and pushes off. You're floating free in space once more. This process is automatic. But it won't be a relaxing ride.

Slow down

Soon, the Soyuz will turn around and fire its engines in a burst of flames called a deorbit burn. This slows the spacecraft, sending it down towards Earth.

There is a *lot* of down between the ISS and Earth.

The ISS is about 4,600 Statues of Liberty high above Earth – the statue is 93m (305ft) from base to torch.

Experts back on the ground have planned a safe landing angle for you. It's time to brace yourself, and trust in the mathematical calculations that your ground support team have done. Here's what happens next...

1. After the deorbit burn, you get rid of the parts of the Soyuz that you don't need for landing. (That's all the parts you're not sitting in.) Expect loud bangs.

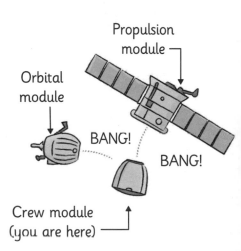

Propulsion module

Orbital module

BANG!

BANG!

Crew module (you are here)

2. The crew module hits the atmosphere. Suddenly, everything's on fire — that's what happens when you rub up against air when falling at thousands of miles an hour. Coming back into the atmosphere is called re-entry. It burns!

3. Your heat shields protect you, and the air slows you down. So while the outside of your capsule gets really, really hot, you'll be fine inside. Enjoy the dramatic flames as they lick against your window.

4. The modules you got rid of will burn up when they hit the atmosphere. Unlike you, their angle of re-entry isn't under control, and they don't have heat shields.

5. Remember the high-G centrifuge from training? You're about to have flashbacks to that as you come in to land. You have been in zero-G for months, but the G-forces of landing are a brutal reminder that life as an astronaut is not all floating around feeling like a feather.

At first, you're pulled down gently into your seat. But, as you descend, that pull gets stronger and stronger, until you feel as though you're about four times heavier than you usually are.

6. Take a moment to be glad at least that your seat stops you from shaking about. You're about to have a truly VIOLENT experience. Thank your carefully-moulded chair for keeping you in one piece.

7. Your 2,000kg (4,400lb) spacecraft is suddenly jarred upwards as a parachute attached to the top of it opens. You'll bounce like a yo-yo. Depending on your personality, this might be the best fun you've ever had, or the scariest thing you've ever done. Or both.

8. The first parachute falls off and another one opens, slowing you down more gently this time. You feel as though you're hanging in the air, the wind whistling outside. You're almost home – landing in 15 minutes.

9. Seconds before you land, your engines fire again, slowing you to a sedate 5km/hour (roughly 3mph).

Then you hit the ground.

Although your seats are designed to absorb the shock, there is still plenty of shock left to go around. Astronauts have described it as feeling like a small car smashing into a truck... and you're the small car. But you're down. You're safe, and you're home. You've also made a considerable mess of the ground where you landed.

Welcome back

The ground crew has been tracking your descent and they're there to welcome you. The hatch opens. Hands reach in to help you out. In Earth's gravity, you feel as though you weigh a ton. You're exhausted. But the fresh air of Earth smells and tastes delicious.

You're carried to a chair and wrapped in blankets. Cameras flash. Someone's handing you a drink. You smile — even though you feel weak — because you've been to space, and now you're back on the beautiful blue-green ball of home.

What do I do when I get home?

After your return to Earth, you'll spend your first days and weeks recovering. Your body will need to build back the muscle and bone you lost in space. But before you rest, you'll take part in welcome ceremonies, where you get to dress up in the national costume of Kazakhstan and receive loads of gifts.

Once you've recovered, you might get a job in Mission Control, or you might start training for your next mission. Some astronauts only ever fly once, while others go to space again and again.

But even one trip will change the way you view the Earth for ever.

> What about the future? Where will humans go next?

That's up to you. Space fans like you can grow up to be the scientists who build rockets to carry people to Mars and beyond. You could be the ones who fly them, or even the ones who settle on alien moons and planets.

What are you waiting for? It's time to prepare. Keep healthy. Study hard. Dream (though not while you're studying). Reach for the stars. (Not literally, they're much too hot.)

The universe is waiting for you...

There are no colonies on other worlds... yet. Perhaps you'll help create the first?

A VERY SHORT HISTORY OF SPACEFLIGHT

1950s
Animals are sent into space to test if it's safe. (Not all of them survive, but enough do for humans to give it a go.)

1961
The first human reaches space, a Russian called Yuri Gagarin. Excellent at spaceflight, not so good at finding a private place to pee.

1965
First spacewalker, Alexei Leonov, risks death when his spacesuit inflates and he can't get back inside. He only manages it by letting some air out.

1969
Humans land on the Moon for the first time. Neil Armstrong and Buzz Aldrin bounce around in the Moon's weak gravity. Millions watch them on television, from the comfort of Earth.

1981
First mission of a new,
plane-shaped, reusable type of
spacecraft called a Space Shuttle.

1986
Tragedy strikes when the crew of the
Shuttle Challenger die in an explosion.

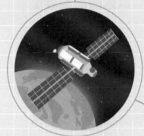

1998
First piece of the ISS is flown into
space in a Russian rocket.

2000
First crew arrives on board the ISS.

2003
Another tragic accident
claims the lives of the crew of
the Shuttle Columbia.

2011
The main construction work on the
ISS is completed. It's also the last
ever flight of a Space Shuttle.

2030s onwards
People who read this book as children
start to become fully-fledged astronauts.

GLOSSARY

Airlock: a two-part door into space that stops air from escaping when an astronaut goes outside.

Atmosphere: the blanket of gases around Earth — that is, the air we breathe.

Cosmonaut: the Russian term for an astronaut.

European Space Agency (ESA): the space agency for all of Europe.

Gravity: a pulling force. Every object pulls on every other object, but the gravity of larger objects is more powerful.

International Space Station (ISS): an orbiting spacecraft where astronauts live and work.

Karman line: a made-up line around Earth that's used as the official boundary of space.

National Aeronautics and Space Administration (NASA): the American space agency.

Orbit: a path around a planet or other large space object, caused by gravity. A spacecraft flying around Earth is described as being 'in orbit' or 'orbiting'.

Soyuz: a Russian spacecraft used as a taxi service to the International Space Station.

Space agency: a government organization in charge of everything to do with space and astronauts.

Zero-G: the 'weightless' feeling astronauts experience in space. Also called microgravity.

Usborne Quicklinks

For links to websites where you can watch video clips of astronauts, explore spacecraft, and find out more about life as an astronaut and how to be one, go to the Usborne Quicklinks website at **www.usborne.com/quicklinks** and type in the keywords 'astronaut's handbook'.

Please follow the internet safety guidelines at the Usborne Quicklinks website.

INDEX

Acknowledgements

Series editor: Lesley Sims
Designed by Jamie Ball
Expert consultants: Libby Jackson
(UK Space Agency) and Stuart Atkinson
With thanks to: Tim Peake (European Space Agency),
Cady Coleman (NASA), Jeremy Curtis and Julia Short
(UK Space Agency) and Margherita Buoso
(European Space Agency)
Photo of Tim Peake on page 5 © Max Alexander/UK Space Agency
Photo of Earth on pages 106-107 © NASA

First published in 2015 by Usborne Publishing Ltd., Usborne House,
83-85 Saffron Hill, London EC1N 8RT, England.
www.usborne.com Copyright © 2015 Usborne Publishing Ltd.